GOD NOW

Janet Zann Sheldon

ISBN 978-1-63844-037-6 (paperback)
ISBN 978-1-63874-578-5 (hardcover)
ISBN 978-1-63844-038-3 (digital)

Christian Faith Publishing, Inc.
832 Park Avenue
Meadville, PA 16335
www.christianfaithpublishing.com

The Scripture quotations contained herein are from the New Revised Standard Version Bible, copyright 1980, by the Division of Christian Education of the National Council of the Churches of Christ in the U.S.A., and are used by permission. All rights reserved.

The quotations used from the Catechism of the Catholic Church are labeled CCC., Copyright 1994, are used with permission from URBI et ORBI Communications.

Printed in the United States of America

To my dear husband, Ron, and our beloved grandchildren.

PREFACE

On the first day of classes in the spring semester of 1969, at Indiana University, my theater professor proclaimed with great enthusiasm, "The best thing in life is to love and be loved!" He repeated this phrase several times with profound passion. I never forgot what he said, but what he didn't say was "How?" How does that happen? How do we make that happen in our lives?

Since that day, I have spent years observing and exploring various world religions and philosophies to learn the path that emphasizes and practices loving and being loved. My exploration eventually led me to the Catholic Christian faith. As time went by, I decided to learn as much as I could about this faith, so I enrolled in a Catholic seminary where I spent four years studying theology. In May 2019, I graduated with a master's degree in Theological Studies. I wanted answers, and I found answers that I will share with you now.

Do you feel like we need God now? Do you feel like God isn't helping us or that you don't know where He is or even *if* He is? If He cares, why doesn't He make the fires, earthquakes, floods, viruses, and other dangerous things go away? What about the people who are

> sick?
> victims of injustice?
> hungry?
> lonely?
> depressed?
> in pain?
> homeless?
> dying?

Why doesn't He answer and help us? Why does there seem to be so much turmoil, chaos, and unhappiness in this country and in the world?

Doesn't He love us? So much is wrong? Why? What are we all supposed to do? How can we have a better life? Where is the love?

Answers

So much uncertainty, so much discontent, so much unknown—and yet these questions and problems can be the beginning of our finding answers and living in peace with God and with each other. So how do we begin?

First

Let us look at God Himself and what He has done and what He continues to do. Then we will look at the reasons that difficult and challenging life problems have come into being. Then we will learn a way to live with love and joy in our hearts, no matter our personal life challenges. We will appreciate God's ways to live and to love that bring joy and life into our very souls and the souls of others.

Be patient. Answers will come if you are open to going beyond the limitations in which your thoughts may have been living heretofore.

God

Within each one of us lives a yearning. A yearning that seeks something beyond ourselves. A yearning that transcends this world. That yearning is for God, our Creator. He created us with this yearning and with the ability to recognize Him as our Creator. This ability makes us capable of communicating with Him and even having a personal relationship with Him.

We know that each person has come from a mother and a father. They, too, came from a mother and a father. When we persevere with this question, we understand that at some time in the history of the human race, the first person was created by a Creator whose existence was of himself, not contingent upon anything or anyone else. We call our Creator, God, who created the universe as we know it.

"Our holy mother, the Church, holds and teaches that God, the first principle and last end of all things, *can* be known with certainty from the created world by the natural light of human reason. Without this capacity, man would not be able to welcome God's revelation. Man has this capacity because he is created 'in the image of God'" (CCC 36). This means that we bear a resemblance to God.

Despite our imperfections, we do recognize truth and goodness and beauty in creatures and creation. These reflect the perfection of God. God is fully spirit and fully love itself. He created the universe and us in it so that He could share love and joy with us. He continues to provide all we need to live throughout our lives.

We have much for which to thank and praise Him. "I will be a father to you, and you shall be my sons and daughters, says the Lord Almighty" (2 Corinthians 6:18).

Okay, then, where is He now?

The short answer is: He *is* with us now.

"Well," you might say, "why isn't He doing more to help us?"

Perhaps it is *we* who need to look to *Him* and learn.

First, He created everything we would need to live. Then he created human beings. He wants us all to know and understand that He is God and believe in Him with great faith and trust. This has been God's desire since He created the first people. We will see that believing in Him and trusting Him include living according to what He knows is best for humankind. Later, we will discuss the topic of evil in the world. First, we will explore the first human creations to understand what God does *for* mankind and what is desired *from* mankind. Our aim is to grow in a relationship with God by noticing his presence and His creations often, along with developing a very thankful heart with which to love Him and offer ourselves to His service. In His love, He made Himself known to our first parents, Adam and Eve.

Paradise Before Fall of Adam and Eve by Brueghel

God's Revelation to Adam and Eve

The Lord God reveals Himself to us, through His revelation to Adam and Eve, His first human creations. He made a beautiful garden where they were comfortable and content. He made them to share life with Him. God spoke to them in the garden and told them they could enjoy any of the trees in the garden except for the tree of the knowledge of good and evil. He said if they ate from that tree, they would die. Eve was tempted and decided to gain the wisdom that God had, so she ate from the tree and shared the fruit with Adam. They both disobeyed God, and God banished them from the garden. Now they were alienated from God. They turned away from God (sinned). Their disobedience resulted in their loss of innocence. Their lives would no longer enjoy all the goodness they had before they disobeyed their Creator. Even Creation itself was affected by their fall. This brought death, disease, earthquakes, famine, and more to our earth.

Due to Adam and Eve's disobedience, all of humanity from that time on is born with human nature "deprived of original holiness and justice" (CCC 404). Their sinfulness (turning away from God) is transmitted to all people. But human nature has not been totally corrupted: it is wounded in the natural powers proper to it. When we are baptized, we receive grace (love) from God which erases original sin and turns mankind back toward God (CCC 405).

An Invitation

All you who are thirsty, come to the water. You who have no money, come, buy grain and eat; come buy grain with no money, wine and milk without cost! Why spend your money for what is not bread; your wages for what does not satisfy? Only listen to me, and you shall eat well, you shall delight in rich fare. Pay attention and come to me; listen, that you may have life. (Isaiah 55:1–3a)

Seek the Lord while he may be found, call upon him while he is near. Let the wicked forsake their way, and sinners their thoughts; Let them turn to the Lord to find mercy; to our God who is generous in forgiving. For my thoughts are not your thoughts, nor are your ways my ways—oracle of the Lord. For as the Heavens are higher than the earth, so are my ways higher than your ways, my thoughts higher than your thoughts. (Isaiah 55:6–9)

What we learn here is that Our Creator offers us all the things that we want: meaning, life, and ultimate joy. He gives us this unconditional love, from His heart and His desire to be close to us. Our role as His creations is to accept His love. He created us to share creation with Him, to share His love and His life and His glory. All that we have was given to us as a gift. This is grace, the free gift of God's love.

> But I, through the abundance of your mercy, will enter your house. I will bow down toward your holy sanctuary out of fear (awe) of you. (Psalm 5:8)

When we accept God's gift of love, we enter into His realm where great love permeates us and everything else. Here we are expected to abide by His ways in everything we are and everything we do. We cooperate with His grace, His love for us. We should not abuse our freedom. In His divine house, we want to cooperate with Him and act like Jesus acts.

It is our duty to listen to what He teaches us and obey. If we decide to do life our own way (be our own god and ignore what He tells us), we miss out on the loving guidance He wants to give us along the path of our life. We live apart from God. By living apart from Him, we lose our relationship with God because our hardened hearts don't listen or obey the Almighty God of love. The good news is that we can turn back to our merciful God. When we turn back to Him, we can reestablish our relationship. We can know that He will help us to realize we were wrong to turn from Him, and that our dependence on Him is a gift that helps us to stay in relationship with Him.

The Church teaches that because of our ancestors' disobedience, each of us lives in a state of concupiscence. This means that we are often tempted to do the wrong things. But thanks be to God, He promises to help us in each and every situation in our lives so that we can stay in good relationship with Him. He is our God of mercy and kindness who desires the very best for us. When we cooperate with Him by living as He teaches, we will live in His peace.

When we make mistakes—and we all do—*and* we are sorry, we can receive the Sacrament of Reconciliation. This is one of seven sacraments where we can experience the presence of God. In this case, we receive His forgiveness.

Perhaps you feel your sins are so grievous that God will not forgive you. The truth is, our God wants and waits to forgive you! By taking responsibility for turning away from God and being sorry that we offended Him, we can participate in this sacrament and receive forgiveness for even grave (mortal) sins. God is faithful in His love and desires that we return to Him. When we are willing to do everything we can not to commit this sin again, we can receive His forgiveness and be assured of His help and love for us. This sacrament restores our relationship of intimate friendship which is love.

Pour out your problems to God. He will share your burdens. Speak (pray) to Him about anything: social life, work life, emotional life, spiritual life. St. Augustine of Hippo (in northern Africa) wrote:

> Great are you, O Lord, and exceedingly worthy of praise: your power is immense, and your wisdom beyond reckoning. And so we men, who are a due part of your creation, long to praise you—we also carry our mortality about with us, carry the evidence of our sin and with it the proof that you thwart the proud. You arouse us so that praising you may bring us joy, because you have made us and drawn us to yourself, and our heart is unquiet until it rests in you.[1]

St. Augustine tells us that our hearts will not rest until they rest in God. Often, we find ourselves pursuing happiness in areas that give us a feeling of power or wealth or prestige. St. Augustine tried all these worldly ways before he finally learned to find happiness obeying and serving the God of the universe.

---

[1] St. Augustine's Confessions (Lib 1.1–2.2.5: CSEL 33, 1–5).

COMING CLOSER TO GOD

You already have God very close to you. You just may not be aware of Him. We can have an actual relationship with the One who is Love itself. We do this by cultivating our hearts in gratefulness to God for all He does for us. Who and what are your most beloved family, friends, and experiences? What comes to your mind that makes you smile in happiness and gratefulness?

Allow your heart to absorb the love that God put in the multitude of gifts that He gives you. Pause…thank Him for your favorite gifts by naming them.

You have now responded to God's love for you. He gives. You respond with thanksgiving. The more you talk (pray) to Him, the more your relationship will grow. He hears you. He loves you; no matter what is going on in your life, He is with you all of the time. Keep thanking Him for all the goodness you can think of. You have that goodness in your life because He provides it. Being thankful is a wonderful way to live. Thankfulness can help your outlook on life. Having an outlook of thankfulness will create smiles on your face and love in your heart for God and for others. This is what makes the world a better place.

It's important to persevere in naming the things you are grateful for to God. There will be days when you don't feel thankful. When this happens, think of things to name and thank Him anyway. They might be small things or situations. Don't change your new mind-set just because of your feelings. Better feelings usually will return when you continue to pray your thankfulness to God. Your outlook can change when you cultivate a strong attitude of thankfulness. Your faith (belief in God) can sustain you, even when your feelings are flat.

Your actions can change your thinking and lead you to a closer and more trusting relationship with your Creator. Don't let feelings bring you down or to despair. The God who made you loves you and wants you to trust Him in all situations. If, of course, your situation is dire, you may need to act to save yourself or others by reaching out to people who can help you. God knows that we need each other and provides help through others. You can also be that help for others if you have the ability to help, even if it is in a small way. Your help is a participation with God to do good for another person. This is love and makes the world a better place.

Love is defined many ways in this world. Real love, true love for another, is willing the goodness for the other. To will the good for another is love. Love is where we take ourselves out of the picture and act for the best for others. When we love others, we also bring love to ourselves.

St. Therese of Lisieux is known for her love. She loved God very much and went into the convent to become a nun like her sisters. She decided by an act of her will that she would make love her vocation. She performed her small duties each day with great love. She decided to smile and show love to all she would meet. She would show the love of God to others through her interactions. She was asked to write down her prayers and communications with God in her spiritual life. Her writings are still widely read all over the world in her book, *The Story of a Soul.* She died at the early age of twenty-four in 1897. She was made a doctor of the Church in 1997.

Saint Therese of Lisieux

St. Teresa of Calcutta wrote a beautiful meditation called "I Thirst for You." It embodies love (The "I" here, is Jesus).

> It is true. I stand at the door of your heart, day and night. Even when you are not listening, even when you doubt it could be Me, I am there. I await even the smallest sign of your response, even the least whispered invitation that will allow me to enter. I know what is in your heart—I know your loneliness and all your hurts—the rejections, the judgments, the humiliations, I carried it all before you. And I carried it all for you, so you might share My strength and victory. I know especially your need for love—how you are thirsting to be loved and cherished. But how often have you thirsted in vain, by seeking that love selfishly, striving to fill the emptiness inside you with passing pleasures—with even greater

emptiness of sin. Do you thirst for love? "Come to me all you who thirst, I will satisfy you and fill you." (John 7:37)

Do you thirst to be cherished? I cherish you more than you can imagine—to the point of dying on a cross for you. I thirst for you. Yes, that is the only way to even begin to describe My love for you. I THIRST FOR YOU. Come to Me and I will fill your heart and heal your wounds. I will make you a new creation and give you peace, even in all your trials I THIRST FOR YOU. You must never doubt My mercy, My acceptance of you, My desire to forgive, My longing to bless you and live My life in you. I THIRST FOR YOU. If you feel unimportant in the eyes of the world, that matters not at all. For Me, there is no one any more important in the entire world than you. I THIRST FOR YOU. Open to Me, come to Me, thirst for Me, give me your life—and I will prove to you how important you are to My heart.

Whatever you do, open the door of your heart. Whenever you come close enough, you will hear me say again and again, not in mere human words but in spirit, "No matter what you have done, I love you for your own sake. Come to Me with your misery and your sins, with your troubles and your needs, and with all your longing to be loved. I stand at the door of your heart and knock. Open to Me, for I THIRST FOR YOU."[2]

---

[2]   A letter written by Mother Teresa (St. Teresa of Calcutta), March 25, 1993. www.aleteia.org.

St. Teresa of Calcutta is teaching of God's personal love for each of us and for us to respond by opening the door of our hearts to Him. God creates us and gives us the gift of free will. He does not force Himself on us. He waits for us to invite Him into our hearts so that we can have a genuine and mutual love relationship.

Saint Teresa of Calcutta

LOOKING BACK

Looking back helps us to know that God and His love existed for us at the beginning. As we learn our early human history, we can appreciate that God created the world and its creatures for good and for love with Him.

God revealed Himself to Moses close to 1250 BC to commission him to lead the Israelites out of Egypt. (The Israelites had been slaves there for four hundred years.) Moses was tending his father-in-law's flock when an angel of the Lord appeared to him as fire flaming out of a bush (Exodus 3:2). God called out to him telling him that He is the God of "Your Father, the God of Abraham, the God of Isaac, and the God of Jacob" (Exodus 3:6). God told Moses that He would be with him as he led them out of Egypt. Moses was surprised to hear God speaking to him and questioned God as to whom he should say sent him. God then replied to Moses, saying, "Tell them I AM has sent you...the LORD, the God of your ancestors has sent me to you" (Exodus 3:14–15).

This tells us that God spoke to Moses personally telling him that He is God. This story of what happened and how God emancipated the Israelites from Egypt is an event of God's love that the Jewish people still celebrate today over three thousand years later. This huge event reveals that God cares about people who are in bondage and that He acts to help them. He speaks. He tells us who He is. He loves us through our difficulties.

Train of Israelites Through the Red Sea by Jordaens

God promises Moses that he will be with him and He was. By fire and a cloud, He physically led the Israelites out of Egypt and eventually into the Promised Land. While the Israelites were camped out near Mount Sinai, God told them that He chose them to be His Chosen People. God spoke to Moses, saying, "This is what you will say to the house of Jacob…if you obey me completely and keep my covenant, you will be my treasured possession among all peoples" (Exodus 19:3–5).

A covenant is an agreement, but *more* than an agreement. A covenant is a deep relational promise between God and man that should never be broken by either party. A covenant is the giving of oneself to another and the other giving himself back to the giver. God is saying that He will be their God and they will be His People.

God then teaches His people what they need to do to live in peace and harmony with each other and with Him. God gave Moses and his brother, Aaron, the Ten Commandments to share with the people:

1. I am the Lord your God. You shall worship the Lord your God and Him only shall you serve.
2. You shall not take the name of the Lord your God in vain.
3. Remember to keep holy the Sabbath day.
4. Honor your father and your mother.
5. You shall not kill.
6. You shall not commit adultery.
7. You shall not steal.
8. You shall not bear false witness against your neighbor.
9. You shall not covet your neighbor's wife.
10. You shall not covet your neighbor's goods.

At this time in history, most people believed in multiple gods. God revealed Himself as the true God and the only God. The Ten Commandments say to us: Love God; Love your neighbor. They are written in the book of Exodus 20:1–17.

There were more laws that the Lord gave to Moses for the people, so they would know how to live as God desired them to live. Moses was obedient and related all the words and ordinances of the Lord. The people replied in one voice, "We will do everything that the Lord has told us" (Exodus 24:3).

Moses went up Mount Sinai and was there for forty days and forty nights. The people below did not know what had happened to Moses, so they asked Aaron to make them a god who would go before them. Aaron did as they asked. The people sacrificed burnt offerings to a golden calf image of god. The Lord God saw the people and told Moses go down the mountain to the people. God was angry that they had turned away from the way He had commanded them. Moses tried to persuade God to remain faithful to the Sinai covenant even though the people had broken it. Moses was successful, and the Lord acquiesced to Moses' wishes. Here God shows us His loving mercy for his beloved people, even after they had hurt Him.

The Lord God next spoke to Moses on the top of the mountain. He came down in a cloud and proclaimed the name, "Lord." He continued, "The Lord, the Lord, a God gracious and merciful, slow to anger and abounding in love and fidelity" (Exodus 34:5–6).

This is God describing himself to mankind. He was telling us his character, so we can trust Him and know beyond a shadow of a doubt that He is God.

The Hebrew Chosen people of God wandered in the desert toward the Promised Land for forty years. They continually wavered between faithfulness and sin. When they reached the Promised Land (today's Israel), God helped them settle in this land of milk and honey. Despite all the help from God, the people did not keep their covenant with God. Many men married women from families that worshipped idols; the men often turned their backs on the true God and worshipped idols with their wives and families. Strong armies came and conquered the tribes of Israel and the people were exiled from the land. Some were eventually allowed to return. All the time that God's people were turning away from him, God sent warnings to his people through the prophets. They warned the people that bad things that were happening to them because of their unfaithfulness to their covenant with God. The prophets also told the people that if they repent and change their ways, God will reward them greatly.

God continues to plead with us even today! He says, "If then My people, upon whom my name has been pronounced, humble themselves and pray, and seek my face and turn from their evil ways I will hear them from heaven and pardon their sins and heal their land" (2 Chronicles 7:14).

In Moses' day, the people refused to persevere in faith to the one true God of their Fathers. They worshipped idols instead. Today, what do we do that God pleads with us still? Could it be worshipping money, fame, ourselves, our things, pornography, gambling, alcohol? Is it God who does evil things or are we committing evil acts against ourselves and Him? What is He saying in the above paragraph that we should do to have our sins pardoned and our land healed?

BEFORE MOSES

Before God made the covenant with the Hebrew people at Mount Sinai, He made a covenant with Adam and Eve. Their unfaithfulness ruined that covenant; peace with God was lost. But in Genesis 3:15, God promises that peace with Him will be restored. He said that the "seed of a woman" would crush the head of the serpent. We believe that "the seed" is Jesus and the "woman" is Mary, His mother. The serpent is Satan. So even at the very beginning of humanity on earth, God knew what He would have to do to save mankind. He knew His love and mercy would bring His children back to Him in the fullness of time.

The second covenant God made was with Noah. Because mankind with his wounded human nature and free will continued to sin (to turn away from the blessings of God and live his own way), God desired to start mankind over again. He chose faithful Noah and his family. Noah obeyed God, and His covenant with Noah was for him and his family to re-populate the world.

The world *was* populated, and around 1850 BC, God appeared to a man named Abram and said, "I am God the Almighty. Walk in my presence and be blameless. Between you and me I will establish my covenant, and I will multiply you exceedingly" (Genesis 17:1b–2). He desired that Abram (who He renamed Abraham), would "become the father of a multitude of nations. I will make you exceedingly fertile; I will make nations of you; kings will stem from you. I will maintain my covenant between me and you and your descendants after you throughout the ages as an everlasting covenant, to be your God and the God of your descendants after you" (Genesis 17:4–7). In Abraham's progeny will come Christ Himself. Also, God will give Abraham the entire land of Canaan as a permanent possession. This was God's third covenant.

Everything that God said would happen did happen. When Moses led the Hebrews out of Egypt, the fourth covenant with the Hebrew people was made at Mount Sinai with the Ten Commandments about 1250 BC.

Around the year 1000 BC, David became King of Israel. God loved David very much. God even said, "He is a man after my own heart" (Acts 13:22). David's family was God's chosen family as revealed by the prophet Nathan in 2 Samuel 7:16, "Your house and your kingdom are firm forever before me; your throne shall be firmly established forever." This was God's fifth covenant.

This tells us that the future Messiah would come from the royal family of David. The two-thousand-year link from Abraham to David to Jesus is outlined clearly in the first chapter of the book of Matthew in the Bible.

THE INCARNATION

God's love and mercy never end. In God's love for humankind, He sent His only Son, Jesus, to be God's "new and everlasting covenant" (Hebrews 8:10) to all people. He is the one anointed by the Father's Spirit in His incarnation. Jesus is the Christ, the Messiah, the anointed one. He was conceived by the Holy Spirit of God and was born from the Virgin Mary. He would be "a light to all nations and people" (Isaiah 42:6). Where Adam and Eve had failed to keep their covenant with God and brought death to the world, Mary and Jesus bring God's love and life everlasting to everyone who will believe on His name. Jesus' life, death, and resurrection is Good News. It brings the world-wide blessing promised to Abraham.

Nativity by Coypel

JESUS' LIFE OF LOVE

Jesus' coming to earth fulfilled all the prophets' promises that a Messiah would come and save us from our sins and show us the way of love. After his childhood, Jesus begins his public ministry by being baptized. He was baptized by John the Baptist as a sign to all people that we must be "born again" of water and the spirit. Just after Jesus was baptized, the Spirit of God descended on him like a dove: "And a voice come from the Heavens saying, 'This is my beloved Son, with whom I am well pleased'" (Matthew 3:17). This introduces Jesus as who He is in relation to God the Father. As His ministry progresses, we learn that He is God, the Son, the second person of the Holy Trinity—He became truly man while remaining truly God.

Baptism is a rebirth of our spirit which makes us children of God. It takes away our original sin and unites us to the Holy Spirit. At the moment of Jesus' baptism by John, God "anointed Jesus of Nazareth with the Holy Spirit and with power, that he might be revealed to Israel as its Messiah. His works and words will manifest him as 'the Holy one of God'" (CCC 438).

After He was baptized, Jesus chooses twelve men to accompany him on his journey of love. He shows them and us His Father's way of love and joy and truth. These twelve men were so convinced of His truth and love for them that each of them (except one) was willing to die defending his faith in Him. These men are called apostles.

His first "sign" (miracle) was at a wedding in Cana. Jesus and his apostles and his mother were present when the wine "ran short" (John

2:3). Mary told Jesus about it. He then told the servers to fill the jars with water. They did. Jesus said for them to take a sample to the head waiter. They did, and the head waiter asked why the family served the best wine last, meaning that this "wine" was better wine than they served at the beginning of the wedding. In doing this, Jesus revealed His glory. The apostles saw this miracle and began to believe in Him.

Jesus cleansed a man who had leprosy. He healed a military officer's servant and told the officer that his faith was greater than even "anyone in Israel" (Matthew 8:10). He cured his Apostle Peter's mother-in-law. Many others came to Jesus "who were possessed by demons, and he drove out the spirits by a word and cured all the sick" (Matthew 8:16).

In the Villages the Sick were Presented to Him by Tissot

One night, Jesus was in a boat with his apostles and a violent storm came up, and the boat was taking on much water. The men were frightened and woke up Jesus who was asleep. He "rebuked the winds and the sea, and there was great calm. The men were amazed and said, "What sort of man is this whom even the winds and the sea obey?" (Matthew 8:23–27).

Christ in the Storm by Rembrandt

After teaching an enormous crowd of people one afternoon, the people were hungry. Jesus' disciples gathered the food they could which consisted of two fish and five loaves of bread. Jesus took the two fish and five loaves, "and looking up to heaven, he said the blessing, broke the loaves, and gave them to the disciples, who in turn gave them to the crowds. They all ate and were satisfied…those who ate were about 5000 men, not counting women and children" (Matthew 14:18–21).

Jesus raised two persons from the dead. Lazarus had died and had been in his tomb for four days. Martha, Lazarus' sister, was very upset and told Jesus that if he had been there, her brother would not have died. "They took away the stone. Jesus raised his eyes and said, 'Father, I thank you for hearing me. I know that you always hear me; but because of the crowd here I have said this, that they may believe that you sent me,' and when he said this, he cried out in a loud voice, 'Lazarus, come out.' The dead man came out, tied hand and foot with burial bands and his face was wrapped in a cloth. Jesus said to them, 'Untie him and let him go'" (John 11:38–44).

"Jairus had a daughter who was twelve years old. She was very sick and died. People at her home wept and wailed over her death. Jesus said to Jairus who was a synagogue official, 'Do not be afraid; just have faith.' He took the girl's parents into her room and took the little girl's hand, saying to her, 'Talitha koum,' which means, 'Little girl, I say to you, arise!' She arose immediately and walked around" (Mark 5:35–42).

Raising Lazarus by Bloch

These signs Jesus did are miracles because they can only be attributed to divine power. Raising people from the dead, calming the seas, and multiplying food substances are actions outside the realm of this earth. They transcend our human abilities and show the power of God in the spiritual world. Jesus does what his Father desires and is both divine and human—divine as his Father is divine and human as we are human. These miracles were done from the love of the Father to accomplish not only what was needed at the time, but also to give us all today, hope and assurance of the power of the love of God through his Son.

After this, Jesus cleansed the Temple (which He referred to as "His Father's house") from the money changers. The people asked for a sign that the Temple was indeed His Father's house. Jesus answered, "Destroy this temple and in three days I will raise it up" (John 2:19).

Jesus was referring to His future Resurrection. He was speaking of his body as being the new and everlasting Temple. Many people began to believe in Him. In fact, "great crowds from Galilee, the Decapolis, Jerusalem, and Judea, and from beyond the Jordan followed him" (Matthew 4:25).

When he saw the crowds one day, he went up the mountain and sat down with his disciples (all those following him including his apostles). He taught them saying:

> *Blessed are the poor in spirit,*
> *for theirs is the kingdom of heaven.*

This means that we should be humble, knowing that all the blessings we have come from God. Humility gives us an inner peace that helps us do the will of God.

> *Blessed are those who mourn, for they shall be comforted.*

When we are sad about our sins and other events in our lives God will comfort us.

> *Blessed are the meek, for they shall inherit the earth.*

This means we should use self-control and be gentle with ourselves and others.

Blessed are those who hunger and thirst for what is right; they shall be satisfied.

This means that when we care about justice and morality and work toward them with passion to do God's will, God will help us to be satisfied with our efforts.

Blessed are the merciful; they will be shown mercy.

If we desire mercy for ourselves, we must also give mercy to others when they need it. We are to treat others always as we wish to be treated, ourselves.

Blessed are the pure in heart; they shall see God.

The Catechism of the Catholic Church 1723 teaches, "The beatitude we are promised confronts us with decisive moral choices. It invites us to purify our hearts of bad instincts and to seek the love of God above all else. It teaches us that true happiness is not found in riches or well-being, in human fame or power, or in any human achievement...but in God alone, the source of every good and of all love."

Blessed are the peacemakers; they shall be called the children of God.

To bring peace to a situation, we need to bring respect, kindness, ears to hear, an understanding heart, and wisdom from God. Prayer to God opens us to His Holy Spirit who can help us to empty ourselves and accept these gifts from God which are ours for the asking.

Blessed are those who are persecuted for the sake of what is right, for theirs is the kingdom of heaven.

Many people have been persecuted for doing what was right. Many of the saints are in this category. All the martyrs have been persecuted for doing what was right in God's eyes. If we are persecuted for doing what we know to be right, God will reward us greatly in heaven.

These eight teachings of Jesus to all the people gathered are called The Beatitudes which mean "blessed" and imply "happiness" will belong to those who follow these teachings. The Beatitudes are God's answer to how we find happiness. He has placed in our human hearts the desire for happiness, and He wants to "draw man to the One who alone can fill it" (CCC 1718).

Let's pause and think about what we have just heard—that Jesus alone can fill our desire for happiness. This means that He knows you as well as you know yourself, and He is telling you what you need to be happy. Rereading the Beatitudes can help us to reset our goals and prayerfully come closer to our Father to live like He lived, with great love and respect for all. When we do this, He promises us the possession of the Kingdom of God (CCC 1716). It is through making God's desires for us our desires for ourselves that we can achieve peace in our hearts.

JESUS' TRANSFIGURATION

Jesus took Peter, James, and John "up to a high mountain by them-selves. And he was transfigured before them; his face shone like the sun and his clothes became white as light. And behold, Moses and Elijah appeared to them, conversing with him" (Matthew 17:1–3). Peter and the other two men saw this and offered to build three tents, one for each, Jesus, Moses, and Elijah. "While Peter was still speak-ing, behold, a bright cloud cast a shadow over them, then from the cloud came a voice that said, 'This is my beloved Son, with whom I am well pleased; listen to him'" (Matthew 17:5). At this, the three disciples fell to the ground in reverence to God speaking. Then Jesus touched them, reassuring them that they didn't need to be afraid. The disciples looked up and saw only Jesus, alone.

This visual and auditory experience shows the magnificence and glory of God shown in Jesus. It also confirms that Jesus is the son of God as God himself spoke for the three disciples to hear. In the paragraph just before the story of the Transfiguration, Jesus said, "The Son of Man will come with his angels in his Father's glory, and then he will repay everyone according to his conduct" (Matthew 16:26). This is another miraculous example of Jesus showing all of us that He is not only human, but also divine in nature. No human can do what happened at this event unless He has divine power.

Transfiguration by Bloch

JESUS' INSTITUTION OF THE EUCHARIST

Jesus knew that "the hour had come to leave this world and return to the Father. He wanted to leave his apostles a pledge of his love, in order never to depart from his own, and to make them sharers in his Passover" (CCC 1337).

The night He was betrayed by Judas, one of his twelve apostles, Jesus instituted the Eucharistic sacrifice of His Body and Blood to perpetuate the sacrifice of the cross throughout the ages until He will come again. He made it very clear that this will be His "true" body and "true" blood and that we should consume Him in this sacrifice of love. This we believe in faith because He is veiled in bread and wine. Though He would depart from us in visible form, He will remain with us "mysteriously in our midst as the one who loved us and gave Himself up for us" (CCC 380–381).

Jesus' Body and Blood "preserves, increases, and renews" (CCC 1392) us to live as Christians and to love Him and one another as He loves us. The Catechism of the Catholic Church assures us that there is no surer pledge or clearer sign of this great hope in the new heavens and new earth "in which righteousness dwells" than the Eucharist. Each time you receive Jesus in the Eucharist, you bring yourself closer to Him and He abides in you (John 6:56). "Life and resurrection are conferred on whoever receives Christ (CCC 1391). The Eucharist separates us from sin; it strengthens our charity and helps us to turn from the things in our lives that are disordered. The Eucharist enables us to live His way of love through His strength.

Consuming Jesus in the Eucharist is receiving His divinity into our own bodies.

The Last Supper by Titian

JESUS' DEATH AND RESURRECTION

The day after Jesus' Last Supper, he was scourged, had a crown of thorns shoved on his head, carried his own cross, was nailed on it, died, and was buried. On the third day, he rose from the dead. We know this because the tomb he was buried in was empty and there was a "great earthquake for an angel of the Lord descended from heaven, approached, rolled back the stone, and sat upon it. His appearance was like lightning and his clothing was white as snow" (Matthew 28:2–3). Mary Magdalene, Joanna, and Mary, the mother of James, came to the tomb to anoint Jesus' body. The angel said to the women, "Do not be afraid! I know that you are seeking Jesus the crucified. He is not here, for he has been raised just as he said" (Matthew 28:5–6). The women were afraid, but very happy. They ran to tell the disciples about Jesus, when Jesus met them and greeted them! They touched his feet and Jesus said to them, "Do not be afraid. Go tell my brothers to go to Galilee, and there they will see me" (Matthew 28:9–10).

The women obeyed Jesus. They told his disciples what they experienced. Then Peter "ran to the tomb, bent down and saw only the burial cloths that had been covering Jesus's body. He left, amazed at what had happened" (Luke 24:12).

Jesus appeared to Peter and Cleopas later that day, and they did not recognize him until he broke bread and gave it to them. When they recognized him, he disappeared from their sight. They quickly went back to Jerusalem to tell the other eleven what had happened. While they were explaining, Jesus "stood in their midst and said, 'Peace be with you'" (Luke 24:36). Jesus showed them his hands and his feet and asked for something to eat. He was given fish, and he ate it in front of them so they would know he wasn't a ghost. Then he explained that his death and resurrection were necessary, and that "repentance, for the forgiveness of sins, would be preached in his name to all the nations, beginning from Jerusalem. You are witnesses of these things. And behold, I am sending the promise of my Father upon you; but stay in the city until you are clothed with power from on high" (Luke 24:47–49).

Jesus' death and resurrection are history's most important events to this day and only when He "comes again in Glory" will the joy of that day be equaled. His death and resurrection prove his love for humanity. There is not a greater gift. His sacrifice of Himself was given from His love for all those who will believe on his name. The Catechism of the Catholic Church 654–655 describes two aspects:

> by his death, Christ liberates us from sin; by his Resurrection, he opens for us the way to a new life. This new life is above all justification that reinstates us in God's grace, so that as Christ was raised from the dead by the glory of the Father, we too might walk in newness of life—the risen Christ himself is the principle and source of our future resurrection: Christ has been raised from the dead. For as in Adam all die, so also in Christ shall all be made alive. The risen Christ lives in the hearts of his faithful while they await that fulfillment…their lives are swept up by Christ into the heart of divine life, so that they may live no longer for themselves, but for him who for their sake died and was raised.

After Jesus' resurrection, He stayed on earth for forty days to show His disciples that He was truly raised from the dead. He also commissioned his Disciples to "Go into the whole world and proclaim the gospel to every creature. Whoever believes and is baptized will be saved; whoever does not believe will be condemned" (Mark 16:15–16). He said they would be able to heal the sick and speak new languages and drive out demons as signs of His truth. Then He was taken up into heaven where He sits at the right hand of God, the Father.

Christ of the Cross, detail by Velazquez

Resurrection of Christ by Bloch

THE HOLY SPIRIT

After the Ascension, the Disciples met together and prayed for the Holy Spirit to guide them. After nine days, "suddenly there came from the sky a noise like a strong driving wind, and it filled the entire house in which they were. There appeared to them tongues as of fire, which parted and came to rest on each one of them and they began to speak in different tongues, as the Spirit enabled them to proclaim" (Acts 2:1–4).

At this time, there were holy Jews from every nation under heaven staying in Jerusalem. Each person heard them speaking in his own language about the mighty acts of God. Peter spoke up and explained that God had raised up Jesus "releasing him from the throes of death, because it was impossible for him to be held by it" (Acts 2:24). Peter explained that God raised Jesus and the Holy Spirit has been poured forth from him who God has made both Lord and Messiah. The people asked what they should do. Peter said, "Repent and be baptized, in the name of Jesus Christ for the forgiveness of your sins; and you will receive the gift of the Holy Spirit…those who accepted his message were baptized and about three thousand persons were added that day" (Acts 2:38–41). This event marks the beginning of the Church. This is called Pentecost.

SUSTAINING LOVE GIVEN TO US BY THE HOLY SPIRIT

When Jesus told His disciples He would be leaving them, He promised they would not be left alone—that He would send the Holy Spirit, the Advocate, the Paraclete to help. Jesus was true to His word. He sent the Holy Spirit who is the third person in the Holy Trinity. He was present at the beginning with God, the Father, and God, the Son. He "proceeds" from the Father and the Son to help us become holy.

The Holy Spirit is always with us to strengthen and reassure us when we ask. When we ask Him to help us to live a holy life, He helps us to have the virtues of love, joy, peace, patience, kindness, generosity, faithfulness, gentleness, and self-control.

The Holy Spirit desires that we listen to God within us as He guides all who love Him to love Him with their whole heart and their whole soul, with all their mind and all their strength so they might love each other as Christ loves them. The followers of Christ are called by God, not because of their work, but according to His own purpose and grace.

> When in faith, we surrender to the Holy Spirit and permit Christ to enter into us we are transformed, recreated, into Christ. We become—without anything of our human nature being destroyed—partakers of the divine nature! This is why Christ was conceived of the Holy Spirit, why God became man—that we may be deified!

Such is the holiness to which we are called: nothing less than our hearts being formed into the very heart of God."[3]

We can pray to the Holy Spirit because He is God, the Holy Spirit, the third person of the Holy Trinity. There is one God—in three persons, God the Father, God the Son, and God the Holy Spirit.

---

[3] Pope Emeritus Benedict XVI. "Holiness Today: The Formation of the Human Heart. Tablet Lecture, October 20, 2011, Cathedral Hall.

THE WAY

The early believers were called Followers of the Way or People of the Way. They lived in community where they shared with one another and worshipped God together. They knew the truth that they had seen and experienced. They were believers in Jesus, that He is the Son of God, and that His ways of living were indeed the truth from God. They knew that the love Jesus had for the people was genuine and that he had performed many signs to prove who He is. They knew their vocation in life was to live as Christ lived, loving God and loving neighbor, forgiving others as God forgives us, helping those who cannot help themselves, sharing whatever they had with those who were in need, and teaching the good news (gospel) of Jesus and His saving power.

They strived to live like Christ and to be like Christ. They worked at becoming holy as He is holy, by loving as He loves.

HOLINESS AS THE WAY TO LOVE

When we believe in the Holy Trinity and love God and others in word and deed, we are Christians. As Christians, we are challenged to be like Jesus in His love for everyone. We aren't expected to save the world, but rather to keep the commandments, and live the Beatitudes, forgiving and loving others as we wish to be forgiven and loved ourselves. Because God loves us first (before we love Him), we open our hearts and minds and love Him! He loves us all the time.

He knows what we are thinking and loves us anyway. No matter our state in life, we are all called to love as He loves and to be close to Him in thoughts, prayer, the way we dress, in the way we speak, and in the little choices we make every moment. This is how we become holy. Holiness is abiding in loving union with God, while allowing this relationship to guide our lives. Jesus proved his love for us by willingly suffering and being crucified for our salvation (reuniting humanity to God through the divinity of Christ). He is worthy of our trust, our awe, our worship, our everything.

Pope Emeritus Benedict XVI said in a speech on April 13, 2011, that holiness is "living the present moment with love toward God and the other." When we open our hearts to God, God will make us holy by being so close to us. We don't earn holiness; it is a gift from God.

Jesus was sent by God to form a new humanity because "The love of God has been poured out into our hearts through the Holy

Spirit that has been given to us" (Romans 5:5). We are called to share in His divinity, to become the dwelling place of God (John 14:23). We are all called to be saints, to imitate Jesus. God inscribed that potential in each of us, so it *is* possible! "We use the synergy of God's grace with our collaboration (moral effort)."[4]

We cannot be holy on our own. We can invite God into our weaknesses to help us. We can pray, read, and learn scripture, participate in the Church's sacraments, attend mass, read about the saints of the Church, and notice God's beauty in his magnificent creation. We can pray the Rosary (the Mysteries of Christ). All these ideas and many more are wonderful responses to God's love for us. These ideas help us to live very, very close to Him. When we live moment by moment with God, we live in spiritual peace and love. We feel His love in all the ways He reaches out to us. Then we share His love with others. It is our joy to share the love He gives to us, with others.

The Church provides seven sacraments each of which is a direct connection to God, through Jesus His Son, and the Holy Spirit, our Helper. These include Baptism, Eucharist, Confirmation, Reconciliation, Marriage, Holy Orders, and the Sacrament of the Sick. Each of the sacraments was revealed through the Holy Bible. These sacraments are holy because God is present in them with us. We need His divine strength given to us through the sacraments. The Eucharist is food for our souls. It is Jesus himself hidden under the guise of bread and wine. The Sacrament of Reconciliation allows us to know that we are forgiven for our sins and to feel forgiven as we experience God through a priest. Baptism erases original sin and makes us actual children of God! Confirmation strengthens our faith through the power of the Holy Spirit. Marriage welcomes God into a couple's union. Holy Orders ordains those who qualify, to become deacons, priests, and bishops. The Sacrament of the Sick is the hand of God touching the participant to heal physically, spiritually, or both.

---

[4] Father Nicholas Cachia. Class notes, "A Call to Holiness," July 2020. St. Vincent de Paul Seminary.

MOTHER ANGELICA

Mother Angelica was a woman who became a religious sister, then an abbess in the Poor Clare order of nuns. Mother Angelica founded the Eternal Word Television Network (EWTN), which has become the largest and most influential Roman Catholic media organization in the United States and the world.

Mother Angelica offers three steps to answering God's call to holiness:

1. Accept God on His terms.
2. Accept ourselves as we are.
3. Accept our neighbor as he is.

She adds, "We were created out of love, by Love, in order to love. We are out of place and misfits when we try to be anything else than what we were created to be—good, loving, joyful, compassionate, kind, understanding, chaste and holy—holy as our heavenly Father is holy."[5]

---

[5] EWTN Global Catholic Network Family Newsletter, October 2009. Number 292. Mother Angelica, Foundress. 5817 Old Leeds Road, Irondale, AL 35210

MORE

*The Gospels (Matthew, Mark, Luke, and John) are the announcement of salvation through Jesus. Jesus is the new Moses who brings the law of the Old Testament to perfect fulfillment and is superior to it. The Law can now be reduced to one commandment which is love. The kingdom is offered to those who will submit freely to the will of God.

*To see Jesus is to see the Father. "Whoever has seen me has seen the Father" (John 14:9).

*"God did not give us a spirit of cowardice but rather of power and love and self-control" (2 Timothy 1:7).

*The Lord God fills our souls with His promises, with His peace, with His hope, His mercy and His love—with everything that He is—even with His own body and His own blood. Why? Because He wants us to share in and enjoy the supreme good. The vocation of the Son and humankind is to receive each other as a gift and become a gift to the other. As God gives to us, each of us is called to bring the life we have received in Christ, to others.

*"I tell you, everyone who acknowledges me before others the Son of Man will acknowledge before the angels of God. But whoever denies me before others will be denied before the angels of God" (Luke 12:8–9).

*His will must be number 1 in our souls, if we want to be truly satisfied. We need to unite our wills with His will. To learn what His will is, ask God to show us and to give us the desire to follow His will in our lives.

*Jesus becomes present to us, and not only present, but shared intimately with us when we accept His body and blood into our own, in the sacrament of Holy Eucharist.

*Know that God is in you if you acknowledge that Jesus came in the flesh and belongs to God. If you do this, you can be assured that you belong to God and that He in you is stronger than the evil one who is in the world (1 John 4:4).

*Don't be afraid when you experience trouble or tribulation. "Take courage, I have conquered the world" (John 16:33).

*If your heart is beating, you have a purpose on earth. You do not belong to yourself. You belong to God. He has high purpose for you and your life.

*God wants you to trust Him, worship Him, and pray to Him. He wants you to pray, believing, and knowing He hears you and loves you. Always pray in the name of Jesus.

WHEN DIFFICULTIES COME

Perhaps you have already experienced great difficulty in your life and are still upset or angry about your circumstances. Maybe you are sick now and are trying to understand "why?"

When difficulties arrive in your life, know that God is there with you. He, too, in Jesus, has experienced the same hardships: anxiety, deep pain, scorn, suffering, and even death on a cross. Jesus tells us not to fall into despair. He knows our pain, and He cares. He wants us to draw close to Him. We remember the pain Jesus suffered on the cross. This is a time to unite our own pain to His. He will help us get through. An opened heart receives and trusts Him in all circumstances. St. Catherine of Siena tells us that "trials lead us to true and perfect patience, so we may realize how fickle and unreliable the world is. This makes us detach our affection from the world and set it on God alone by means of pure virtue. For every hardship endured for love of God is rewarded. Its fruit is kept for us in everlasting life."[6]

Saint Catherine of Siena continues to teach that those who live their faith consider every affliction to be a time to come closer to God in trust and loving dependence. When our faith meets the darkness of evil or injustice, suffering or death, we can pray in faith for God to give us peace. We pray often. We look to the witnesses of faith (the Fathers of our faith and the Saints) to persevere in belief despite not "seeing" answers immediately. We can persevere with patience knowing that God has won the battle of suffering and death. "In the

---

[6] Saint Catherine of Siena, Doctor of the Church. Magnificat magazine, Meditation of the Day-*Sharing in Christ's Passion*. Saturday, 28th, p.377.

light of the Resurrection, glory radiates from the place of suffering, of agony accepted in the faith of Christ."[7]

The question of "evil" being allowed to exist is important. Five answers surface:

1. God gave us free will so that humanity and He could enjoy a true and genuine relationship of love. He wants us to choose to love Him as He loves us. When we do not choose wisely, there are natural and sometimes unpleasant consequences. We could choose to drive too fast, or drink too much, or do or say unkind things to another. In many cases our own sinful choices lead to car accidents, ill health, family and friend relationship problems, et cetera. When we choose to be like Adam and Eve and misuse our freedom to disobey the goodness of God's will for us, we bring upon ourselves unpleasant results. God gives us freedom to choose between good and evil.

2. Evil will never have the last word over us, as both the first and the last word over humanity is Jesus Christ, who conquered evil, sin, and death by His Death and Resurrection.

3. Good can come from evil. God can permit evil for the purpose of drawing a greater good from it (like allowing Lazarus to die, but to be raised again, by the glory of God (John 11:4).

4. Lack of knowledge because we cannot know the whole of God's plan as to why He permits evil.

5. Redemptive suffering is suffering, accepted in faith and in unity with Christ on the cross, can earn indescribable graces of healing and salvation for us and others.[8]

---

[7] Mother Marie des Douleurs, Foundress of the Benedictine Sisters of Jesus Christ. Magnificat magazine, Meditation of the Day-In Honor of the World Day of the Sick. Tuesday, 11, p,153.

[8] Father Kevin J. O'Reilly, St. Joseph's Seminary, Yonkers, New York. Essay, "The Problem of Evil" Magnificat Magazine.

"Those who do evil will be cut off, but those who wait for the Lord will inherit the earth" (Psalm 37:9).

We have the Good News that Jesus overcame death. He rose from the dead; his death brings us life. It shouts to us of his love for us; a love that will never die, but triumphs over evil and death.

DRAWING CLOSE TO GOD

The Rosary is a beautiful prayer to pray daily. I look forward to praying it every day. The Rosary takes us through the mysteries of Jesus: his conception, his birth, baptism, and ministry, are several of them. It is a very grounding prayer of truth and love which draws us into the various phases of his life, death, and resurrection.

To pray the Holy Mysteries of the Rosary, follow the directions on the next page as you proceed by first holding the Crucifix, then the beads indicated for each prayer. The specific prayers are written on the following page.

How To Pray The Holy Rosary

1. Make the Sign of the Cross- In the name of the Father, and of the Son, and of the Holy Ghost. Amen
    Then say "The Apostles' Creed"
2. Say the "Our Father"
3. Say 3 "Hail Mary"
4. Say the "Glory Be", then "Fatima Prayer" announce the First Mystery; then say the "Our Father"
5. Say 10 "Hail Marys" while meditating on the Mystery
6. Say the "Glory Be", then "Fatima Prayer", announce the Second Mystery; then say the "Our Father"
7. Say 10 "Hail Marys" while meditating on the Mystery
8. Say the "Glory Be", then "Fatima Prayer", announce the Third Mystery; then say the "Our Father"
9. Say 10 "Hail Marys" while meditating on the Mystery
10. Say the "Glory Be", then "Fatima Prayer", announce the Fourth Mystery; then say the "Our Father"
11. Say 10 "Hail Marys" while meditating on the Mystery
12. Say the "Glory Be", then "Fatima Prayer", announce the Fifth Mystery; then say the "Our Father"
13. Say 10 "Hail Marys" while meditating on the Mystery

Say the "Glory Be", then "Fatima Prayer", then say the "Our Father", say the "Hail Holy Queen"

ROSARY PRAYERS

Apostle's Creed. I believe in God, the Father Almighty, Creator of heaven and earth and in Jesus Christ, His only Son, our Lord; who was conceived by the Holy Spirit, born of the Virgin Mary, suffered under Pontius Pilate, was crucified, died, and was buried, He descended into hell; the third day He arose again from the dead; He ascended into heaven, and is seated at the right hand of God, the Father Almighty, from thence He shall come to judge the living and the dead. I believe in the Holy Spirit, the Holy Catholic Church, the communion of saints, the forgiveness of sins, the resurrection of the body, and life everlasting. Amen.

Our Father. Our Father, Who art in heaven, hallowed be Thy Name. Thy Kingdom come, Thy will be done on earth, as it is in heaven. Give us this day our daily bread, and forgive us our trespasses as we forgive those who trespass against us. And lead us not into temptation, but deliver us from evil. Amen.

Note: After the first bead of the Rosary (which is an Our Father), are three beads in a row that indicate three Hail Marys for an increase in faith, hope, and charity (love).

The Hail Mary. Hail Mary, full of grace, the Lord is with thee; blessed art thou amongst women, and blessed is the fruit of thy womb, Jesus. Holy Mary, Mother of God, pray for us sinners now and at the hour of our death. Amen.

The Glory Be. "Glory be to the Father, and to the Son, and to the Holy Spirit. As it was in the beginning, is now, and ever shall be, world without end. Amen."

Fatima Prayer. O My Jesus, forgive us our sins; save us from the fire of Hell. Lead all souls to heaven, especially those in most need of Thy mercy. Amen.

Hail Holy Queen Prayer. Hail Holy Queen, Mother of Mercy, Our life, our sweetness and our hope. To thee we do cry, poor banished children of Eve. To thee we do send up our sighs, mourning and weeping in this valley of tears. Turn then, most gracious Advocate, thine eyes of mercy toward us, and after our exile, show unto us the blessed fruit of thy womb, Jesus, O clement, O loving, O sweet Virgin Mary. Pray for us O holy Mother of God, that we might be made worthy of the promises of Christ. Amen.

Guide to Days on which to pray specific Mysteries:

Sunday and Wednesday Mysteries to Pray (Glorious Mysteries):

1. The Resurrection (after three days Jesus rose from the dead. He defeated death. He appeared to his disciples, and after 40 days He ascended into Heaven where He sits at the right hand of God the Father Almighty. Jesus will come to earth again, but it will be to judge our lives. Now is the time for us to ask and receive His mercy for our sins.)

2. The Ascension into Heaven (Jesus gave his disciples the power to forgive sins and promised He would remain with them forever. Then He extended His hands, gave them a blessing and ascended into Heaven.)

3. The Sending of the Holy Spirit (Jesus promised His disciples that His Father would send the Advocate, the Holy Spirit, who will teach and remind them of all He has told them (John 16:13).

4. The Assumption of Mary ((following her death God assumed Mary into Heaven.)
5. The Crowning of Mary, Queen of Heaven (because Mary is the mother of Jesus, King of Kings, she is honored as Mother of God and Queen of Heaven.).

Monday and Saturday Mysteries to Pray (Joyful Mysteries):

1. The Annunciation (the announcement from the Angel Gabriel to Mary, and her answer which was yes.)
2. The Visitation (Mary went to visit her cousin, Elizabeth, for several months. Elizabeth was also pregnant with John the Baptist.)
3. The Nativity (the birth of Jesus)
4. The Presentation (Mary and Joseph take Jesus to the Temple to consecrate Baby Jesus to the Lord.)
5. The finding of Jesus in the Temple. (For three days Mary and Joseph couldn't find Jesus after the feast of the Passover that was in Jerusalem.)

Tuesday and Friday Mysteries to Pray (Sorrowful Mysteries):

1. The Agony in the Garden (Jesus prayed in the Garden to the Father. His apostles kept falling asleep. He was deeply troubled but prayed for the Father's will to be done.)
2. The Scourging at the Pillar (Pilate took Jesus and had Him scourged.)
3. The Crowning with Thorns (The soldiers of the governor stripped Jesus and put a scarlet robe on Him and a crown made of thorns on His head and mocked Him.)
4. The Carrying of the Cross (Jesus had to carry His own cross to the hill where He would be killed.)
5. The Crucifixion (Jesus was killed by nailing Him to the cross.)

Thursday Mysteries to Pray (Luminous Mysteries):

1. Jesus' Baptism in the Jordan River by John the Baptist.
2. The Wedding at Cana (Jesus performs a miracle of turning water into wine after the wedding hosts had run out of wine.)
3. The Proclamation of the Kingdom (Jesus preaches the coming of the Kingdom of God. It is the beginning of His ministry of mercy and love which He continues until the end of the world.)
4. The Transfiguration (Jesus was transfigured in light at Mount Tabor. God commands the apostles who were with Him to listen to Him.)
5. The Institution of the Eucharist (Jesus offers His body and blood as food under the signs of bread and wine, at His last supper before being crucified.)

MIRACLES TO CONSIDER

A little more than two thousand years ago, the angel Gabriel "was sent from God to a town of Galilee called Nazareth, to a virgin betrothed to a man named Joseph, of the house of David, and the virgin's name was Mary. The angel said, 'Hail, favored one! The Lord is with you'" (Luke 1:26–28). The angel told her not to be afraid, that she had found favor with God, and that she would "conceive in her womb and bear a son whom she shall name Jesus. He would be great, and his kingdom will have no end. Mary said, 'Behold I am the handmaid of the Lord. May it be done to me according to your word'" (Luke 1:38).

This was Mary's fiat (her yes to the Lord). She agreed to cooperate with God. This was the beginning of her very present collaboration "with the whole work her Son was to accomplish. She is the new Eve, the Mother of the Church, who continues in heaven to exercise her maternal role on behalf of the members of Christ" (CCC 973, 975). She is not a goddess. She is worthy of honor and veneration but not worthy of worship which is to be given to God alone. She rejoiced in God, her Savior as she stated the Magnificat ("Behold I am the handmaid of the Lord. May it be done to me according to your word") because Jesus saved her from sin from the moment of conception. In other words, her sinlessness was a gift of grace, saving her before she sinned. Mary's title, Queen of heaven, was based on the honor of being the Queen Mother of Jesus, the King of kings and the Son of David. She is our spiritual mother.

The next three signs (miracles) open our minds to the beauty and power of Mary's continuing collaboration with her Son to bring humanity to a loving and trusting relationship with Him.

OUR LADY OF GUADALUPE

Spain's Hernando Cortez conquered Mexico City in 1521. Two years later, Franciscan missionaries came to evangelize the Indigenous people. The Aztecs had been offering human sacrifices to their gods. Many, many people were victims of their practices. Juan Diego was a poor Indigenous man who had converted to Catholicism approximately five years before his miraculous meeting occurred.

Near a barren hill called Tepeyac, an area north of Mexico City, on December 9, 1531, Juan Diego was walking to Mass when he heard "beautiful music and saw a beautiful lady who called him by name. Her dress shone as the sun, as if vibrating, and the stone where she stood, as if shooting rays, her splendor was like precious stones, like a jewel. The ground dazzled with resplendence of the rainbow in the fog. Even the foliage appeared like emeralds, turquoises, and gold."[9] The woman identified herself, "I am the perfect and perpetual Virgin Mary, Mother of Jesus, the true God, through whom everything lives. I am your merciful mother, the merciful mother of all of you who live united in this land, and of all mankind. Here I will hear their weeping, their sorrow, and will remedy and alleviate all their multiple sufferings, necessities, and misfortunes."[10] She told Juan Diego to go and tell the Bishop of her wish to build a shrine raised in her honor on the hill.

Juan did as she asked, but the Bishop was unconvinced. Juan returned to the hill where he told Mary what occurred. She told him

---

[9] Julie Carroll. Story of a miracle: Our Lady appears to St. Juan Diego. Sept.29, 2011.thecatholicspirit.com

[10] Father William Saunders. Saint Juan Diego and Our Lady. www.catholiceducation.org/en/culture/catholic-contributions/saint-juan-diego-and-our-lady.html

to try again. This time, the Bishop asked for a heavenly sign from the Virgin to convince him. Once again, Juan related the Bishop's answer to Mary. Mary told Juan that she would give him a sign the next day.

On that next day, Juan did not go to meet Mary. Instead, he went to seek a priest to hear his dying uncle's confession. On his way to find a priest, he saw the Virgin Mary. She assured Juan that his uncle had been healed, and that at the top of Tepeyac hill, he would find what the Bishop requested. Juan climbed the dry hill and saw it full of beautiful roses "like those grown in Castille, but foreign to Mexico."[11] He took off his cloak (tilma) and placed them inside it. When Juan arrived at the Bishop's house, the tilma was opened. The Bishop and his assistants fell to their knees in amazement and profound reverence. They saw no flowers, but the beautiful image of the Virgin Mary emblazoned on the tilma.

The imprint of Our Lady of Guadalupe includes a black cross on the gold brooch at her neck, which is identical to the one emblazoned on the banners and helmets of the Spanish soldiers, as if telling the Aztecs that her religion was synonymous with that of the conquerors. The blue-green hue of her mantle is the same color as that worn by Aztec royalty. "Hence, she is considered by the Aztecs to be a queen, since only the Emperor wears this color."[12] The tilma is made of ayate fiber, a coarse fabric derived from the threads of the maguey cactus plant. The lifespan of the ayate fiber is approximately twenty years. Yet after almost five hundred years, the tilma does not show even the slightest sign of decay. Scientists have declared that there is no coloring of any kind in the fibers of the tilma. The materials used to produce these colors remain unknown to science, being neither animal, vegetable, nor mineral dyes. Furthermore, a microscopic examination revealed that there are no brush strokes, indicating that the tilma is not a painting. Today, almost five hundred years later, this image remains and is framed and displayed in Mexico City's Basilica

---

[11] Ibid.

[12] "Our Lady of Guadalupe Explained." Steubenville Press 2013. 980 Lincoln Avenue, Steubenville, Oh 43952. www.STEUBENVILLEPRESS.COM/ POS-F306D

of St. Mary of Guadalupe, one of the world's most visited Catholic shrines, with tens of thousands of pilgrims coming to visit each year.

This event brought about the conversion of over nine million Aztecs from the worship of false gods. The Bishop authorized construction of a shrine to honor the apparition of Mary.

John Paul II canonized Juan Diego (declared him a saint) near Mexico City in July 2002.

Our Lady of Guadalupe

OUR LADY OF LOURDES

Our Lady of Lourdes refers to the Blessed Virgin Mary, Mother of Jesus, who appeared in the grotto of Massabielle, near Lourdes, France, to a fourteen-year-old girl, Bernadette Soubirous. The year was 1858. On February 11, Bernadette was outside collecting firewood for her family when "she heard a strong wind, then saw a girl about 16 or 17 dressed in a white robe with a blue ribbon tied around her waist, and bare feet with a yellow rose on each foot and rosary beads on her arm. At first no one believed Bernadette when she told them what had happened. Bernadette then disobeyed her mother and even the chief of police in her town and returned to the grotto and had a total of eighteen visions over the next five months. On the ninth visit an underground stream with healing power was revealed. The lady told Bernadette to 'drink from the fountain and bathe in it.'"[13]

Bernadette said that the Virgin made a spring flow from the cave. She also requested that pilgrimages be made to a chapel at this particular site. On the twelfth visit, twenty thousand people came to this area where Bernadette was. The Virgin told her that she was the "Immaculate Conception." This was a term that helped to convince the town's authorities that Bernadette was telling the truth. The virgin also said, "I do not promise to make you happy in this world but in the other."[14] She also gave Bernadette a message for all: "Pray and do penance for the conversion of the world."[15]

---

[13] Miracles of Lourdes. www.olrl.org/stories/ Our Lady of the Rosary Library 11721 Hidden Creek Road, Prospect, KY 40059.
[14] Ibid.
[15] Ibid.

Lourdes is now a world center for pilgrimages. Thousands of people have claimed to be cured in the baths there. The Church has investigated and approved devotion to Our Lady of Lourdes. A medical bureau was established in 1882 to test the authenticity of the cures. To the present date of 2020, sixty-seven physical cures have been substantiated by the Church. Two very amazing miraculous cures were Gabriel Gargam and John Traynor.

Bernadette became a nun in the town of Nevers for the last thirteen years of her life. She died on April 16, 1879. She was declared Blessed in 1925 and a Saint in 1933.

Immaculate Conception

OUR LADY OF THE ROSARY

Our Lady of the Rosary refers to the Blessed Virgin Mary who appeared to three shepherd children once a month for six months on the thirteenth day of each month, beginning on May 13, 1917, and ending on October 13, 1917. The three children were Lucia, age ten, and her cousins, Francisco, age nine, and Jacinta, age seven. The children were tending their sheep at Cova da Iria, a field owned by Lucia's family, in central Portugal, in Fatima (seventy miles northeast of Lisbon).

Due to a coming storm and several flashes of lightning, the three children started for their home. They quickly gathered their sheep and started down the hill. After a "shaft of light split the air, they took a few steps to the right and there standing over the foliage of a small holm oak they saw a most beautiful lady, dressed in white, more brilliant than the sun."[16] The lady told the children not to be afraid and that she would not harm them. Lucia asked where she was from; the lady replied that she is from heaven. Lucia asked what the lady wanted of her. The lady said that she came to ask them to come there for six consecutive months, on the thirteenth day, at the same hour (about noon). Lucia asked if she and Jacinta and Francisco would go to heaven. The lady said they would, but Francisco would have to say many rosaries. Then the lady asked if they would like to offer themselves to God "to endure all the sufferings that He may be pleased to send, as both an act of reparation for the sins with which He is offended and an act of supplication for the conversion of sinners. Lucia answered, 'Yes, we do.' The lady replied, 'Well then,

---

[16] John de Marchi, I.M.C., The True Story of Fatima. A Complete Account of the Fatima Apparitions. http://www.fatimacrusader.com/truestory/pdf/tspg5.pdf

you will have much to suffer. But the grace of God will be your comfort.'"[17]

Then the Lady opened her hands and "shed upon the children a highly intense light, that was as if it were a reflection shining from them." Lucia reported that the light penetrated them to the heart, and it allowed them to see themselves in God, who was that light.

Then the Lady spoke reminding the children to pray the Rosary every day to bring peace to the world and to end the war (WWI). After the Lady left, the children said they felt physical strength and courage and joy.

Lucia wanted to keep the Lady a secret, but young Jacinta couldn't help telling her mother. The word spread to Lucia's parents and family who thought she made up the entire experience with the Lady. Her mother accused her of lying and was very angry with her. Only Jacinta's and Francisco's father believed they were telling the truth.

The second apparition occurred as the children were told on June 13, 1917. When asked by Lucia what the Lady wished of them, she answered, "I want you to pray the rosary every day, and learn to read."[18] Then Lucia asked her if she would please take them to heaven. She replied that she would take Jacinta and Francisco soon, but Lucia would have to remain here for some time in order to establish devotion to her Immaculate Heart in the world. The Lady promised salvation to those who embrace it. Lucia was worried that she would have to stay here alone. The Lady said that she would never forsake her; her immaculate heart will be her refuge and road that leads her to God.

When the children were home again, they were treated as if they were guilty of lying. Their priest told them that this was the work of the devil. They were very upset. More people in the town were hearing that the three children were seeing apparitions of Mary. Most disbelieved.

On July 13, 1917, the children went to Cova de Irea as before and prayed the rosary while they waited for Our Lady. She appeared

---

[17] Ibid.
[18] Ibid.

as before, and when Lucia asked what she wanted of her, Our Lady replied that she wanted them to continue praying the rosary every day in honor of Our Lady of the Rosary in order to obtain peace for the world and end the war. Lucia also wanted to know who she was and if she would perform a miracle so everyone will believe that she appears. Our Lady said to keep coming there every month, and in October, she will tell them who she is and what she wishes and that she would perform a miracle that everyone will see so as to believe.

Then Our Lady asked the children to make sacrifices for sinners, and "say often, O Jesus, this is for love of Thee, for the conversion of sinners, and in reparation for offences committed against the Immaculate Heart of Mary."[19] Then she opened her hands and showed the children a vision of Hell. Lucia described the vision later to the Bishop of Leiria:

> The rays of light seemed to penetrate the earth, and we saw as it were a sea of fire. Plunged in this fire were demons and souls in human form, like transparent burning embers, all blackened or burnished bronze, floating about in the conflagration, now raised into the air by the flames that issued from within themselves together with great clouds of smoke now falling back on every side like sparks in huge fires, without weight or equilibrium, amid shrieks and groans of pain and despair, which horrified us and made us tremble with fear. (It must have been this sight which caused me to cry out, as people say they heard me). The demons could be distinguished by their terrifying and repellent likeness to frightful and unknown animals, black and transparent like burning coals. Terrified we looked up at Our Lady, who said to us, so kindly and so sadly: "You have seen hell where the souls of poor sinners go. To save them, God wishes to establish

---

19 Ibid.

71

in the world devotion to my Immaculate Heart. If what I say to you is done, many souls will be saved and there will be peace.[20]

After the vision, she gave another prayer to help sinners: "When you pray the Rosary, say after each mystery: O my Jesus, forgive us, and save us from the fire of hell. Lead all souls to heaven, especially those who are in most need."[21]

When it was time for the fourth apparition, the children were kidnapped by the county magistrate so he could scare them into saying they were lying about the Lady. The children did not do as he wanted. Eventually, they were able to go home. Two days later, they went to Cova da Iria where the Lady appeared to them. She appeared again September 13, asking as usual for the children to pray the rosary every day to obtain the end of the war. The Lady promised that in October, the Lord would also come, as well as Our Lady of Sorrows and St. Joseph with the child Jesus to bless the world.

Word spread over the area of Fatima and far beyond. Thousands of pilgrims came to try to see the apparition of the Virgin Mary for her sixth and final appearance. Some estimate the crowd to have been seventy to a hundred thousand.

She appeared and said that she would like a chapel to be built here in her honor. She said, "I am Our Lady of the Rosary. Continue to say the rosary every day. The war will end soon, and the soldiers will return to their homes."[22] A little later, she proclaimed, "People must amend their lives and ask pardon for the sins. They must not offend Our Lord any more for He is already too much offended."[23] As Our Lady began to leave the children,

she opened her hands which emitted a flood of light. While she was rising, she pointed toward

---

[20] Ibid.
[21] Ibid.
[22] Ibid.
[23] Ibid.

the sun and the light gleaming from her hands brightened the sun itself. Then the sky was clear. The sun was now pale as the moon. To the left of the sun, Saint Joseph appeared holding in his left arm the Child Jesus. Saint Joseph emerged from the bright clouds only to his chest, sufficient to allow him to raise his right hand and make, together with the Child Jesus, the Sign of the Cross three times over the world. As Saint Joseph did this, Our Lady stood in all Her brilliancy to the right of the sun, dressed in the blue and white robes of Our Lady of the Rosary. The sun had taken on an extraordinary color. The words of the eyewitnesses best describe these stupendous signs.

We could look at the sun with ease; it did not bother us at all. It seemed to be continually fading and glowing, throwing shafts of light one way and another, painting everything in different colors, the people, the trees, the earth, even the air. Everyone stood still and quiet, gazing at the sun. Then the sun seemed to dance until it seemed to loosen itself from the skies and fall upon the people. At that point some people begged for mercy. It looked like a revolving ball of fire falling upon the people. Finally, the sun swerved back to its orbit and rested in the sky. Everyone gave a sigh of relief. The miracle had come to pass.[24]

Francisco and Jacinta did go to heaven while they were still children as Our Lady promised them. Lucia became a nun and lived until 2005 when she died at the age of ninety-seven.

---

[24] Ibid.

These are three examples of divine spiritual life communicating with our earthly lives. This kind of communication is analogous to God communicating to His prophets so they could share His truths with the people. It is true that we do not see many of the spirits, but as with the Holy Spirit Himself these are genuine. The angels and saints; Mary, Jesus, Joseph; the Holy Spirit; and the Communion of Saints participate with God and for God, when He deems it necessary for our good.

Our Lady of Fatima by Chambers

THE CHURCH FATHERS

The following are quotes from the early Church fathers who lived within a century or two to Jesus and his apostles. Many of the Church fathers are just two generations away from the apostles who were actually *with* Jesus.

Origen (AD 182–AD 254), in a commentary on St. Matthew's Gospel, 16, 23:

> Every spiritual being is by nature, a temple of God, created to receive into itself the glory of God.

Origen, Fifth Homily on Leviticus, 2:

> Here then is what God Almighty says of you—I mean of humanity: "I will live in them and move among them." (2 Corinthians 6:16)

Gregory of Nazianzen (AD 329–AD 390) (Eulogy of Basil, the Great, Oration 43, 48) quotes Basil of Caesarea as saying that: "The human being is an animal who has received the vocation to become God."

Gregory of Nazianzen, Dogmatic Poems, 8:

> The Word of God took a lump of newly created earth, formed it with his immortal hands into

our shape, and imparted life to it: for the spirit that he breathed into it is a flash of the invisible Godhead. Thus, from clay and breath was created humanity, the image of the Immortal… That is why in my earthly nature I am attached to life here below, while I also have in me a portion of the Godhead; therefore, my heart is tormented by the desire for the world to come.

Gregory of Nyssa (AD 335–AD 394), On the Creation of Man, 11:

An image is not truly an image if it does not possess all the characteristics of its pattern… It is characteristic of divinity to be incomprehensible: this must also be true of the image. If the image could be essentially understood while the original remained incomprehensible, the image wouldn't be an image at all. But our spiritual dimension, which is precisely that wherein we are the image of our Creator, is beyond our ability to explain… by this mystery within us we bear the imprint of the incomprehensible Godhead.

Gregory of Nyssa, Second Homily on the Song of Songs:

Know to what extent the Creator has honored you above all the rest of creation. The sky is not an image of God, nor is the moon, nor the sun, nor the beauty of the stars, nor anything of what can be seen in creation. You alone have been made the image of the Reality that transcends all understanding, the likeness of imperishable beauty, the imprint of true divinity, the recipient of beatitude, the seal of the true light. When you turn to him you become that which he is himself... Nothing in creation can be compared with your greatness. God is able to measure the whole heaven with his span. The earth and the sea are enclosed in the hollow of his hand. And although he is so great and holds all creation in the palm of his hand, you are able to hold him, he dwells in you and moves within you without constraint, for he has said, "I will live and move among them." (2 Corinthians 6:16)

These quotations go deep into theology, explaining:

*your importance to God;
*we are immortal and have the opportunity to live with God forever through all eternity;
*our spirit holds the very imprint of God; and
*we are honored by God above all His other creatures, because we can hold Him in ourselves!

Finally

Jesus was with God at the beginning. He sees our sin and from His love for us, He enters human history. He enters into a world of evil and death which He embraces so that He becomes one with His beloved people. He gives us Himself which is hope and new life. His love is a special, unique love for each one of us, and it is forever. No end. He overcame death, and when we say yes to Him with our heart and soul, we, too, will overcome death. Our Lover desires for us to become One with Him, Our Beloved.

Through the Holy Spirit we are restored to paradise, led back to the kingdom of heaven, and adopted as children, given confidence to call God, "Father" and to share in Christ's grace, called children of light, and given a share in eternal glory.[25]

GOD NOW? Yes, we can have God now, and we can have Him forever. The better question is: Will *we* choose Him?

---

[25] CCC 736. St. Basil, De Spiritu Sancto, 15, 36: PG 32, 132.

AFTERWORD

Carry Me!

"Carry me!"

"Pardon me, I couldn't hear you."

"Carry me!" four-year-old Michelle pleads.

"Okay, I'll try," I say as I struggle to lift her. Her body weight is growing, and my arm strength is not. I manage to lift her, and as she feels comforted, she drops her head to rest on my shoulder. Oh! What a wonderful feeling it is to feel her rest on me as I carry her. Her wanting to rest on my shoulder feels like she loves and trusts me; I feel an indescribable love for her.

After a few minutes, my strength is depleted. I put her down but reassure her that I should be able to pick her up again in a few minutes. She counts down two minutes, and I pick her up again and carry her. Together, we both enjoy wonderful feelings of loving and being loved.

This example of mutual love and respect is very much like the love our Creator desires to have with each one of His children. There are days when even we as adults would like to be "carried" by our loving God—to share our burdens with Him and know that He understands and will help us to receive rest and reassurance that everything will be all right.

Early this morning, I had one of those feelings. I opened my daily devotional book by Sarah Young, *Jesus Calling*, for reassurance. (She has one page for each day). It said, "Seek to live in my love… wear my love like a cloak of light, covering you from head to toe.

Have no fear, for perfect love decimates fear… My Love will once again envelop you in light… Rest in Me, My Child…"

Allowing myself to relax with God's reassurance that I am safe with Him, I prayed the Rosary as I rested in peace, feeling a new loving appreciation of Mary, our Mother, and Jesus, her Son, our Lord and Savior.

ABOUT THE AUTHOR

Janet Zann Sheldon has recently written GOD NOW to explore and provide answers to some of life's toughest questions. Her University of Michigan master's degree in educational psychology coupled with her St. Vincent de Paul Catholic Seminary master's degree in theological studies serve as the foundation for her work. She has taught and counseled children and adult students over four decades, helping them to grow in knowledge, strength, and love. Today, she wishes to inspire you by sharing information that will encourage you in your faith journey. Janet enjoys swimming, reading, walking on the beach, and being with her family (especially her grandchildren).

CPSIA information can be obtained
at www.ICGtesting.com
Printed in the USA
BVHW050440011221
622869BV00017B/700